SUPERSTARS OF WRESTLING

Beth Phoenix

By Ryan Nagelhout

Gareth Stevens Publishing

D1300743

Please visit our website, www.garethstevens.com. For a free color catalog of all our high-quality books, call toll free 1-800-542-2595 or fax 1-877-542-2596.

Library of Congress Cataloging-in-Publication Data

Nagelhout, Ryan.
 Beth Phoenix / Ryan Nagelhout.
     p. cm. — (Superstars of wrestling)
 Includes index.
 ISBN 978-1-4339-8513-3 (pbk.)
 ISBN 978-1-4339-8514-0 (6-pack)
 ISBN 978-1-4339-8512-6 (library binding)
 1. Phoenix, Beth, 1980—Juvenile literature. 2. Women wrestlers—United States—Biography—Juvenile literature. I. Title.
 GV1196.P52N34 2013
 796.812092—dc23
 [B]
                               2012029061

First Edition

Published in 2013 by Gareth Stevens Publishing
111 East 14th Street, Suite 349
New York, NY 10003

Copyright © 2013 Gareth Stevens Publishing

Designer: Nicholas Domiano
Editor: Ryan Nagelhout

Photo credits: Cover background Denis Mironov/Shutterstock.com; cover, pp. 15, 25 Ethan Miller/Getty Images Entertainment/Getty Images; pp. 5, 11 Moses Robinson/Getty Images Entertainment/Getty Images; p. 7 Jim R. Bounds/AP Images for WWE; p. 9 max blain/Shutterstock.com; pp. 13, 21 Miami Herald/McClatchy-Tribune/Getty Images; pp. 17, 29 ALEXANDER KLEIN/AFP/Getty Images; p. 19 © iStockphoto.com/Paha_L; p. 23 AP Images/Marc Serota); p. 27 Helga Esteb/Shutterstock.com;

Printed in the United States of America

CPSIA compliance information: Batch #CW13GS: For further information contact Gareth Stevens, New York, New York at 1-800-542-2595.

Contents

Meet Beth

Beth Phoenix is a wrestling superstar!

Beth was born Elizabeth Kocanski on
November 24, 1980, in Elmira,
New York.

7

Beth became a wrestling fan when she was little. She watched matches with her grandmother on the weekend.

Drawing Interest

When Beth was 11, she won a coloring contest. Her prize was tickets to her first live wrestling match. She fell in love with the sport!

First Matches

Beth went to Notre Dame High School in Elmira. She was the school's first female varsity wrestler!

Beth was a great amateur wrestler. In 1999, she won the North-East wrestling title. She also won at the New York State Fair.

Beth became a professional wrestler in 2000. She traveled to events on weekends while going to college in Buffalo, New York.

17

Big Debut

In 2005, Beth signed with the WWE.

She made her debut on May 8, 2006,

disguised as a fan.

19

Phoenix Rises

On October 7, 2007, Beth beat

Candice Michelle to win the WWE

Women's title!

In 2008, Beth and Santino Marella beat Mickie James and Kofi Kingston in a tag team match. Beth took back her WWE title and has dominated women's events ever since.

23

The Big Hurt

Beth has had several injuries in her career. In 2006, Beth broke her jaw during a match. She has also battled major ankle injuries. She's tough!

Stopping Bullies

Beth is taking a stand against bullies. In 2011, she and other WWE members joined the Be a STAR Alliance. This group helps stop bullying in schools.

Beth Phoenix

Natalya

27

What's Next?

Beth's wrestling career is still taking off!

What will she do next?

29

Timeline

1980	Elizabeth Kocanski is born on November 24.
1991	Beth goes to her first live wrestling match.
1999	Beth is the first female varsity wrestler at her high school.
2005	Beth signs with WWE.
2006	Disguised as a fan, Beth makes her WWE debut.
2007	Beth wins her first WWE Women's title.
2011	The WWE joins the Be a STAR Alliance.

For More Information

Books:

Black, Jake. *The Ultimate Guide to WWE*. New York, NY: Grosset & Dunlap, 2011.

Websites:

Beth Phoenix Online

bethphoenixonline.net/
Check out this great source for Beth Phoenix information on the web.

Beth Phoenix's WWE Page

wwe.com/superstars/divas/bethphoenix
The official WWE site for photos, videos, and information about Beth Phoenix.

Online World of Wrestling

onlineworldofwrestling.com/profiles/b/beth-phoenix.html
Keep track of Beth Phoenix's matches with this recap.

Glossary

amateur: not competing for pay

career: the job that someone chooses to do for a long time

debut: a first official public appearance

disguise: to mask or hide

dominate: to be the best, have the best position, or have control

injury: something that causes pain or damage

professional: earning money from an activity

varsity: the main team representing a college, school or club in contests

Index